Tokyo is not for tal
extremes, where   il-
lity meets speed.
tory, Tokyo's mod   e
developed into a   whilst
remaining distinctly Japanese. With 35 million people crowding
the city, there's always an adventure to be had.

CITIx60: Tokyo explores the Japanese capital in five aspects, cover-
ing architecture, art spaces, shops and markets, eating and entertainments. With expert advice from 60 stars of Tokyo's creative
scene, this book guides you to the real attractions of the city for
an authentic taste of Tokyo life.

Contents

Before You Go

BASIC INFO

Currency
Yen (JPY/¥)
Exchange rate: $1 : ¥100

Time zone
GMT +9
Japan does not observe DST.

Dialling
International calling: +81
Citywide: 03

Weather (avg. temperature range)
Spring (Mar–May): 11–19°C / 52–66°F
Summer (Jun–Sep): 22–29°C / 72–84°F
Autumn (Oct–Nov): 12–20°C / 54–68°F
Winter (Dec–Feb): 3–11°C / 37–52°F

USEFUL WEBSITES

Train routes, schedules & fare
www.hyperdia.com

Japan Meterorological Agency
www.jma.go.jp/en/quake/

EMERGENCY CALLS

Ambulance, fire or emergency rescue
119

Police
110

If a quake occurs, open the door to secure an exit and seek shelter under a table. After the first tremors, turn off the stove, keep calm and evacuate. Turn on a radio for news.

Embassies / consulates
China   +81 (0)3 34 03 33 88
France   +81 (0)3 57 98 60 00
Germany   +81 (0)3 57 91 77 00
UK   +81 (0)3 52 11 11 00
US   +81 (0)3 32 24 50 00

AIRPORT EXPRESS TRANSFER

Narita Airport <–> Tokyo Station (Narita Express)
Trains / Journey: every 15–30 min / 60 min
From Narita Airport – 0730–2144
From Tokyo Station – 0618–2003
One-way: ¥3,020
www.jreast.co.jp/e/index.html

Haneda Airport <–> Tokyo Station (Monorail)
Trains / Journey: every 3–5 min / 25 min
From Haneda Airport – 0511–0005
From Tokyo Station (JR Yamanote Line) – 0450–2352 (Change @Hamamatsu-cho Station)
One-way: ¥650
www.tokyo-monorail.co.jp/english/haneda

PUBLIC TRANSPORT IN TOKYO

Rails, Metro, Monorails
Bus
Taxi

Means of Payment
SUICA / PASMO smart cards*
JR Pass (unlimited travels within timed periods)
Cash

*Both SUICA and PASMO cover JR, metro, rails within Tokyo, and almost all bus routes.

PUBLIC HOLIDAYS

January	1 New Year's Day, Coming of Age (2nd Mon)
February	11 Foundation Day
March	Vernal Equinox Day
April	29 Showa Day
May	3 Constitution Memorial Day, 4 Greenery Day, 5 Children's Day
July	Marine Day (3rd Mon)
September	Respect-for-the-Aged Day (3rd Mon), Autumnal Equinox Day
October	Health and Sports Day (2nd Mon)
November	3 Culture Day, 23 Labour Thanksgiving Day
December	23 Emperor's Birthday

Shops and museums normally close on Jan 1 or during Dec 24–Jan 3.

FESTIVALS / EVENTS

February
Japan Media Arts Festival
j-mediaarts.jp

March
Art Fair Tokyo
artfairtokyo.com
Fashion Week Tokyo (also in October)
tokyo-mbfashionweek.com
Tokyo International Anime Fair
www.tokyoanime.jp

April
Hanami (Cherry Blossoms Festival)
Roppongi Art Night
www.roppongiartnight.com
Tokyo TDC Exhibition
tdctokyo.org/eng

May
Design Festa (also in November)
designfesta.com

July
Sumidagawa Fireworks Festival
sumidagawa-hanabi.com

August
Summer Sonic
www.summersonic.com
Yokohama Triennale (through to November)
www.yokohamatriennale.jp

September
Tokyo Art Book Fair
zinesmate.org

October
Tokyo Designers Week (through to November)
www.tdwa.com
Tokyo International Film Festival
www.tiff-jp.net
Trans Arts Tokyo (through to November)
kanda-tat.com

Event days vary by year. Please check for
updates online.

UNUSUAL OUTINGS

HATO BUS Tokyo Night Tour
www.hatobus.co.jp

Haunted Tokyo Tours
www.hauntedtokyotours.com

Tokyo Great Kayaking Tour
www.facebook.com/tokyokayak

Yako Night Cruise Tour (#55)
www.keihinferry.co.jp/event/factory.html

Walk Japan
www.walkjapan.com

SMARTPHONE APP

Art & cultural event listings
TokyoArtBeat

Speech to speech translator
NariTra

Rail & subway routes & station locator
Tokyo Rail Map+ Lite

REGULAR EXPENSES

Newspaper
¥100–200

Domestic / International mail (postcards)
¥50 / 70

Gratuities
Good service is standard practice in Japan.
Tipping can cause embarrassment.

Count to 10

What makes Tokyo so special?

Illustrations by Guillaume Kashima aka Funny Fun

Never tired of innovating, Tokyo dazzles the eye in so many ways.
Respect for tradition fuses with zest for new ideas, and reality and
fantasy worlds converge. In places you are just as likely to meet
groups of costumed anime fans as you are office workers. The city
feels alive with new ideas and creative expression. Whether you are
on a one-day stopover or a week-long stay, see what Tokyo creatives
consider essential to see, taste, read and take home from your trip.

1

Architecture

Harajuku Church
by Ciel Rouge Création

Yoyogi National Gymnasium
by Kenzo Tange

**Tokyo Metropolitan
Government Building**
by Kenzo Tange

St. Mary's Cathedral
by Kenzo Tange

Nakagin Capsule Tower
by Kisho Kurokawa

Prada Aoyama Epicenter
by Herzog & de Meuron

Tama Art University Library
by Toyo Ito

Za-Koenji Public Theatre
by Toyo Ito

SELFIES @ EDO-TOKYO ARCHITECTURAL MUSEUM

OHA!

MEET TOTORO @ GHIBLI MUSEUM OR MAYBE Mʳ MIYAZAKI HIMSELF!!!

?!?

ATARASHII...

NANYODO BOOKS

2

Contemporary Art Museums & Galleries

Edo-Tokyo Open Air Architectural Museum
www.tatemonoen.jp

Museum of Contemporary Art Tokyo
www.mot-art-museum.jp

Hara Museum of Contemporary Art
www.haramuseum.or.jp

3331 Arts Chiyoda
www.3331.jp

TOTO Gallery
www.toto.co.jp/gallerma

GA Gallery
www.ga-ada.co.jp

TARO NASU GALLERY
www.taronasugallery.com

3

Cartoon Classics

Ghibli Museum
www.ghibli-museum.jp

Fujiko F. Fujio Museum
fujiko-museum.com

Gundam Front Tokyo
gundamfront-tokyo.com

Kitaro Chaya
www.youkai.co.jp

Osamu Tezuka's grave
Shinjuku-ku

Anpan-man Children's Museum (Yokohama)
www.yokohama-anpanman.jp

J-World
www.namco.co.jp/tp/j-world

4

Art Books & Magazines

Nanyodo Books
nanyodo.co.jp

UTRECHT / NOW IDeA
www.nowidea.info

PAPER WALL Shinagawa
www.paperwall.jp

SO BOOKS
www.book-oga.com

Totodo
totodo.jp

B&B
bookandbeer.com

PARCO Book Center
Shibuya Parco Part 1, B1F-15-1, Udagawa-cho, Shibuya-ku

Book 1st Shinjuku
www.book1st.net

5

Nourishment

Fresh sea produce
Tsukiji Market (Sushi Dai)
www.tsukiji-market.or.jp

Superb sushi
Sukiyabashi Jiro
www.sushi-jiro.jp

Curry rice
CURRY UP®
curryup.jp

Steak & hamburg steak
Meat Yazawa Gotanda Tokyo
www.kuroge-wagyu.com/my

Baked cheese tarts & cakes
Pablo
www.pablo3.com

**Tonkatsu
(breaded, deep-fried pork)**
Tonki
1-1-2, Shimo-Meguro, Meguro-ku

6

Coffee Breaks

Crafted tableware & manga
Café Zenon
www.cafe-zenon.jp

Maid café
@home Cafe
www.cafe-athome.com

All things chocolatey
100&ChocolateCafe
www.choco-cafe.jp

Café x event space
a-bridge
www.a-bridge.jp

Botanical boutique x treehouse
Biotop
www.biotop.jp

Film & Television Studio x Café
Soulplanet
www.soulplanet.jp

7

Snacks &
Instant Food

**Imoyokan
(sweet-potato paste)**
Funawa
funawa.jp

**Senbei / Shikibunosato
(rice crackers)**
*www.shikibunosato.com/
hikaru.html*

Freshly deep-fried croquettes
Togoshi Ginza Shotengai (#36)

Onigiri (rice ball)
7-11, Lawson or Familymart

Freeze-dried Japanese food
Amano Foods
www.amanofoods.co.jp

Ekiben (bento box)
Ekiben Matsuri
www.nre.co.jp

8

Leisure

View the city from the Inner Circular Route expressway

Watch firework displays
Sumidagawa Fireworks Festival, Tokyo Bay Grand Fireworks Festival, Jingu Gaien Fireworks

Stroll around Jinbocho for rare art books & have Napolitan (pasta) at Saboru Café 1
1–11, Kanda Jinbocho, Chiyoda-ku

Drink coffee gyunyu (coffee with milk) in a sento after a bath

Get lost in the city by bike

Try out intelligent toilets at department stores

9

Entertainment

Join a PechaKucha event
at SuperDeluxe (#51)
www.pechakucha.org

Enjoy a show
at Robot Restaurant (#48)

Go bowling with glowing balls & black-light lanes
EST Shibuya Bowling
www.shibuyaest.co.jp

Enter an Edo-themed hot spring bath
Oedo Onsen
www.ooedoonsen.jp/daiba

Spend a day at amusement park
Tokyo Dome City
www.dukeellington.com

Explore Hong Kong's defunct Kowloon Walled City in Tokyo
WAREHOUSE KAWASAKI
www.warehouse.co.jp

10

Mementos

Local folk crafts
Bingoya
www.quasar.nu/bingoya

Curated ceramic wares
PASS the BATON
www.pass-the-baton.com

Daily necessities
Tokyu Hands / Loft
shibuya.tokyu-hands.co.jp
www.loft.co.jp

Antique kimono fabrics
Asakusa flea markets

Wagashi
HIGASHIYA GINZA (#28)

Sensu (traditional folding fan)
Bunsendo
1-20-2, Asakusa, Taito-ku

Icon Index

 Opening hours   Admission

Address   Facebook

 Contact   Website

 Remarks

 Scan QR codes to access Google Maps and discover the area around each destination. Internet connection required.

60x60

60 Local Creatives x 60 Hotspots

From vast cityscapes to the smallest snippets of conversation, there is much to inspire creative urges in Tokyo. 60x60 points you to 60 haunts where 60 arbiters of taste develop their nose for the good stuff.

Landmarks & Architecture   SPOTS · 01 – 12 📍

Get lost in a scrapbook-like cityscape where traditional and cutting-edge architecture blends. Then clear your mind in a zen garden or an age-old shrine.

Cultural & Art Space   SPOTS · 13 – 24 📍

Open eyes and mind to Tokyo's far-reaching cultural offerings. Traditional handicrafts to boundary-pushing contemporary arts define the capital's dynamism and character.

Markets & Shops   SPOTS · 25 – 36 📍

From pricey high fashion to cheap home accessories, old art books to new gadgets, shopping here is all encompassing. Get ready to take a part of Tokyo home.

Restaurants & Cafés   SPOTS · 37 – 48 📍

Tokyo is replete with imaginative ramen, fresh made sushi, hearty stews and moreish snacks on sticks. The city's baristas are dedicated to purist coffee craft.

Nightlife   SPOTS · 49 – 60 📍

Whether your taste is for whisky, wanton clubbing or whiling away time with your novel, you'll find a befitting late-night haunt.

Landmarks & Architecture

Cultural icons, historic shrines and public spaces

Both the 1923 Great Kanto earthquake and fire bombings in WWII caused massive destruction to Tokyo's traditional architecture resulting in a pulsating contemporary landscape. The city's architecture is a celebrated example of Tokyo's forward thinking ideology. Solidifying its reputation as a modern hub, buildings continually push boundaries, and sleek materials, angular shapes and colossal height dominate.

Tokyo is infamous for sky rise buildings, with around 50 buildings standing taller than 180 metres, a phenomenon that gained momentum after a 31-metre height limit was abolished in 1963. Though futuristic buildings dominate the city, remnants of traditional architecture can still be discovered. At the Imperial Palace, remains of the Edo Castle, built in 1590, can still be seen. For architecture verging on the bizarre, visit the Nakagin Capsule Tower (*8-16-10, Ginza, Chuo-ku*) a disjointed building built in 1972 by Kisho Kurokawa (1934–2007), that resembles a pile of huge washing machines stacked one on top of the other. A visit to the Reiyukai Shakaden (*1-7-8, Azabudai, Minato-ku*) reveals a pyramid constructed out of black granite, built in 1925 which houses a reservoir of 400 tonnes of water, to be used as an emergency source if Tokyo meets with some kind of disaster.

LESLIE KEE
Fashion photographer

Born in Singapore and represented by Super Sonic. I directed SUPER in 2004 and won Minister Prize for Tiffany's charity book. My book, *SUPER LOVE*, will be out at my 15th work anniversary.

Yokohama Osanbashi P.015

Eisuke Tachikawa
Founder, NOSIGNER

NOSIGNER is a design firm dedicated to identifying and solving problems. Our initiatives to solve practical and social problems have gained critical acclaim across the globe.

Kosuke Oho
Creative director, WOW

WOW is a visual design studio based in Japan and UK. WOW's recent projects include visual direction for fashion shows, live music performances, and art events.

TOKYO TOWER P.014

TOKYO SKYTREE® P.016

DYSK
Commercial photographer

I'm born in Osaka and raised all over Japan with a good eye for the finer things in life. I spent my 20s abroad and have been to six continents.

Kokyogaien P.020

Shun Kawakami
Art director & artist, artless Inc.

Born in Tokyo in 1977, I've been actively involved in a wide-ranging creative endeavours, such as branding, interactive, video, product, installation, and spatial design.

Kashiwa Sato
Art director

I founded SAMURAI and have drawn up NACT's logo, Uniqlo's brand strategy, and Fuji Kindergarten. I also authored KASHIWA SATO'S *Ultimate Method for Reaching the Essentials*.

Meiji Jingu P.017

The National Art Center, Tokyo P.021

NIGO®
Fashion designer, producer & DJ

NIGO® directs HUMAN MADE, and designs for EFFECTOR by NIGO® and film *IMPOSSIBLE* by NIGO®. He also established curry eatry CURRY UP® and spins music at TERIYAKI BOYZ®.

Nihon
Mingeikan
P.023

Lucas Badtke-Berkow
Founder, Knee High Media

Born in Baltimore in 1971 and raised in San Francisco, I came to Japan in 1993 to found Knee High Media Japan. Published magazines include *Tokion*, *Mammoth*, *Papersky*, and *Plants*.

Makie Kubo
Editor, IDEA

Editing is for books inspired by people, but for shops and galleries I like, the owner's personality comes first. I also edit publications other than graphic design magazine *IDEA*.

Ginza
Kabukiza
P.022

Myojin Yu
P.024

Nezu
Museum
P.026

Toshiyuki Takei
Producer, TOKYO

I work at an advertising production firm – that's why I often get to visit and learn about wonderful places. My projects span from TV commercials and music videos, to other film-related works.

Takeshi Hamada
Graphic designer

Born in 1970, I went to Germany in 1999 and am now based in Tokyo. I founded online magazine *Tiger* in 2000. My work was published in Pyramyd Éditions' collection "design&designer."

Keizo Kuroda
Hair & make-up artist

I style hair and design make-up for TV commercials, music videos, and other film-related works.

Namiyoke
Inari Jinja
P.025

Saiko
Saibansho
P.027

1 TOKYO TOWER
Map I, P.106

Erected during Japan's postwar boom, TOKYO TOWER is an enduring mark of the country's economic success. Formally the city's radio and analogue television transmitter (until TOKYO SKYTREE® (#3), the Eiffel Tower-inspired structure still looms over Tokyo in its iconic orange and white, sending a warm neon glow across the city as dusk darkens the sky. Observation decks at 150m (MO) and 250m (SO) offer views across the Kanto region and, southeast, as far as Mount Fuji.

🕐 0900–2200 daily (SO: –2130)
💲 ¥1,600/1,000/800 (MO+SO)
🏠 4-2-8, Shibakoen, Minato-ku
📞 +81 (0)3 34 33 51 11 🔗 www.tokyotower.co.jp

"TOKYO TOWER is the symbol of the Olympic games of the past and the future now the games are coming back to Tokyo for 2020!"
– LESLIE KEE

2 Osanbashi Yokohama
Map T, P.111

"Osanbashi" is Japanese for "big pier." Built in 1894, the structure is the oldest pier in Yokohama. Its current form of curved surfaces and large column-free space is the result of a grand prize-winning reconstruction project initiated in 1994, in which UK-based Alejandro Zaera-Polo and Farshid Moussavi stretched the pier's capacity to accommodate four 30,000-tonne ships at once. Visit the wooden observation deck to soak up the sun's rays off the Bay or a gleam rooftop view of Yamashita Park and surrounding CBD, Minato Mirai.

🕐 Rooftop & 1F parking: 24hrs, 2F: 0900-2130
🏠 1-1-4, Kaigandori, Naka-ku, Yokohama   ☎ +81 (0)4 52 11 23 04
URL www.osanbashi.com/en

"The night view is especially beautiful. Sometimes, you can see a rainbow made of overlapping neon light."

– Eisuke Tachikawa, NOSIGNER

3 TOKYO SKYTREE®
Map M, P.109

TOKYO SKYTREE® is the capital's newest centrepiece and broadcasting tower. At 634m, the white earthquake-proof structure boasts being the tallest free-standing tower in the world. A digital 19th-century mural at the entrance references the capital's history (the figure, which reads "6(mu)-3(sa)-4(shi)" in Japanese, also denotes the region's historical name, Musashi), while two viewing decks, the TOKYO SKYTREE TEMBO DECK (350m) and the TOKYO SKYTREE TEMBO GALLERIA (450m) allow 360° views of today's modern city.

🕐 0800-2200 daily   💲 ¥2,060/1,540/930/620
(TEMBO GALLERIA: +¥1,030/820/510/310)
🏠 1-1-2, Oshiage, Sumida-ku
📞 +81 (0)3 53 02 34 70   🌐 www.tokyo-skytree.jp

"This is a straightforward and definite spot to go. Get a splendid view of Tokyo from its observation decks."
– Kosuke Oho, WOW

4 Meiji Jingu

Map A, P.102

Emperor Meiji, the great-grandfather of the present emperor, modernised Japan in the 19th and early 20th century. To honour his virtue, this shinto shrine was built in 1920 and dedicated to the divine spirits of Emperor Meiji and his consort. Exit at Harajuku station. The gateway here leads to *naien* (inner precinct), a serene area with manmade forest and shrine buildings that locals flock to on New Year's Day to make their first prayer of the year. About 2km away, *gaien* (outer precinct) in Aoyama promotes sports and culture. Enjoy autumn scenery on its Gingko-lined street.

🕓 From dawn to dusk
🏠 1-1, Yoyogikamizonocho, Shibuya-ku
📞 +81 (0)3 33 79 55 11
URL www.meijijingu.or.jp

"It's unbelievably peaceful here, particularly in the early morning when there are less people around. Feel the seasons here smack in the middle of Tokyo."

– DYSK

5 Kokyogaien
Map I, P.107

This striking setting inhabits the former site of Edo Castle, which was reconstructed as the Imperial Palace in 1888, only to be destroyed in WWII. Shortly afterwards, the palace was rebuilt to the exact measurements of the initial structure and continues to house Japan's Imperial Family. A short walk from Tokyo station, *Kokyogaien*, the Imperial Palace Plaza, is surrounded by moats and colossal stonewalls and occupies 3.41 square kilometres in total. The compound's inner grounds are rarely open to the public but visit on January 2 (New Year's Greeting), December 23 (Emperor's birthday), or during cherry blossom season for exclusive inside access. Otherwise, reserve a guided tour.

⌂ 1-1, Kokyogaien, Chiyoda-ku
☏ +81 (0)3 32 31 55 09
URL www.env.go.jp/garden/kokyogaien/english
⏀ Free guided tour: 1000 (M–F except P.H.), 1330 (M–F, Sep–Jul 20), 18+, sankan.kunaicho.go.jp/english/about/koukyo.html

"Experience Japanese sense of beauty here. The quiet evenings at Imperial Palace are my favourite moments in Tokyo."

– Shun Kawakami, artless Inc.

6 The National Art Center, Tokyo (NACT)

Map D, P.104

NACT, the Suntory Museum of Art in Midtown and the Mori Art Museum in Roppongi Hills collectively form a major cultural hub, known as "Art Triangle Roppongi." When celebrity architect Kisho Kurokawa (1934-2007) planned the centre, he envisioned an oasis of comfort amid the intense urban district. Contorted glass curtains and huge inverted cones are among ornaments designed to create confusion, inviting visitors to ponder architecture as they might art. Visit in the late afternoon when the sun is about to set for awe-inspiring views.

🕐 1000-1800 (W-M & P.H., except Wednesdays after P.H. Tuesdays), -2000 (Fridays during exhibitions) 🅂 Admission varies with programmes 🏠 7-22-2, Roppongi, Minato-ku 📞 +81 (0)3 57 77 86 00 URL www.nact.jp

"At its shop 'Souvenir From Tokyo,' you will find, as its name suggests, a perfect souvenir from Tokyo. Goods include original stationery, tableware and clothing."

– Kashiwa Sato

7 Ginza Kabukiza

Map I, P.107

Embracing the architectural style of its prede-
cessors, Kabukiza Theater's fifth manifestation
by Kengo Kuma has remained a hallmark for
kabuki dance drama since opening in 1889.
Elegant features of the last Momoyama-style
design built in 1951 by Yoshida Isoya (1894–1974)
are skillfully preserved, with improved acces-
sibility. Also designed by Kuma on the site is
a distinctive 29-storey office building at odds
with the overall design. A full *kabuki* programme comprising three to four act dance-
dramas from different plays spans hours, while
last-minute tickets for single acts sell at the
ground-floor ticket counter. Also see Kuma's
bamboo-covered tearoom on the fifth floor.

🕐 1100–, 1630– (Full-day)
💲 Ticket price varies with seating
🏠 4-12-15, Ginza, Chuo-ku
URL www.kabuki-za.co.jp
🎧 Earphone guide: ¥700,
Cash only for single-act tickets

*"The new theater just unveiled in spring 2013.
Enjoy a kabuki performance with English earphone
guide, as well as its architecture."*
– NIGO®

8 Nihon Mingeikan
Map A, P.102

Also known as Muneyoshi Yanagi in Japan, Soetsu Yanagi (1889–1961), the philosopher that made *"Mingei"* (daily necessities made by common folks using local materials), personally designed *Nihon Mingeikan* (The Japan Folk Crafts Museum) in 1936, right next to his own home. It's possible to extend your museum visit to the house, where Yanagi's designer son, Sori Yanagi (1915–2011), also lived during his childhood, every second and third Wednesday and Saturday.

🕐 1000–1700 (Tu–Su & P.H. except Tuesdays after P.H. Mondays)
💲 ¥1,100/600/200
🏠 4–3–33, Komaba, Meguro-ku
📞 +81 (0)3 34 67 45 27
URL www.mingeikan.or.jp/english

"Experience a real Japanese lifestyle as you take off your shoes to enter the museum."

– Makie Kubo, IDEA

9 Myojin Yu

Map C, P.103

The healing properties of this traditional Japanese-style *sento* (public bath) are known to avail muscle aches, pains, and sore joints whilst providing relaxation. With its 16th century architecture, the majestic structure resembles a temple, and the site has been used frequently in movies and commercials. Visitors are met with equally beautiful features inside. Vibrant hand-painted walls surrounding the herbal baths depict Japanese landscapes.

🕐 1600–2330 daily except 5th, 15th, 25th of each month & the day after P.H.) 💲 ¥450/180/80
🏠 5-14-7, Minamiyukigaya, Ota-ku
📞 +81 (0)3 37 29 25 26
🔗 www.ota1010.com/yu.cgi?no=059,code=e

"Bring a towel, soap and shampoo. Go there in daytime as beautiful light comes through the windows. The artwork on the walls is amazing!"

– Lucas Badtke-Berkow, Knee High Media

10 Namiyoke Inari Jinja
Map I, P.107

Built in 1657, this little shinto shrine is cherished by fishmongers and fishermen working at nearby Tsukiji, one of the world's largest fish markets. The construction of the land beneath the shrine, originally on the water's edge, was susceptible to crashing waves. The water did not calm until the workers floated an *Inari* in the sea. Now the shine's role is to safeguard the area, perfectly lending itself to its literal translation: "Protection from the waves." Set aside an hour or so to inspect the quirky monuments hidden on site, and look out for a little stall where you can have your fortune read.

🕐 24hrs daily,
Main building: 0500-1700 daily
🏠 6-20-37, Tsukiji, Chuo-ku
☎ +81 (0)3 35 41 84 51
URL www.namiyoke.or.jp

"Come in June to join their big festival where people carry Mikoshi (portable shrine)."

– Toshiyuki Takei , TOKYO

11 Nezu Museum

Map A, P.103

Founded in 1914 and renovated by architect Kengo Kuma in 2009, the new Nezu Museum is a graceful integration of tradition and urban design. Dark pitched roofs and glass walls set off railroad baron Kaichiro Nezu's (1860–1940) collections and donations of over 7,400 Japanese and oriental antiquities against a splendid leafy garden where colours change by season. Stroll in the garden, especially around mid-May when the abundance of blooming irises appears to dye the pond purple, then unwind at peaceful modern tearoom NEZUCAFÉ. Carefully curated exhibitions rotate seven times a year.

🕙 1000-1700 (Tu–Su & P.H. except Tuesdays after P.H. Mondays) 💲 ¥1,000/800, Special exhibition: ¥1,200/1,000 🏠 6-5-1, Minami-Aoyama, Minato-ku 📞 +81 (0)3 34 00 25 36 🔗 www.nezu-muse.or.jp

"This is the place to feel the spirit of Japan from both the collections and appearance."

– Keizo Kuroda

 Saiko Saibansho

Map I, P.106

Being the first western-style Supreme Court in the country, the impressive landmark was envisioned by Shinichi Okada in 1974, winner of an open competition among runners-up Kenzo Tange and Yoji Watanabe. Running parallel to its neighbouring National Theatre and National Diet Library, the Brutalist concrete structure is said to be partially inspired by the U.S. Supreme Court, with corridors and staircases held between hollowed-out walls. No photography is allowed inside.

🏠 4-2, Hayabusacho, Chiyoda-ku
☎ +81 (0)3 32 64 81 51
URL www.courts.go.jp/english

"This building has no curves and makes a great graphic impact. You won't want to go there for official business. Just to admire its look."

– Takeshi Hamada

Cultural & Art Space

Newfangled galleries, reputable museums and cultural projects

With an all-inclusive arts and cultural offering, Tokyo champions the experiments of young emerging artists as well as the traditional art forms, creating a fusion of contemporary influence and century old ritual.

Since 1998, a law giving art initiatives freedom from government restrictions has enabled a daring and diverse arts landscape that continues to evolve. Now, over 750 galleries are located in the capital, usually called 'Kashi-garo' or 'Kikaku-garo' ('garo' means 'gallery'). The former is a kind of rental gallery where artists rent a space for an exhibition, whereas Kikaku-garos are curator-run galleries working on commission. As such, expect to see a plethora of experimental exhibits often tucked out of the main thoroughfare. Japan's largest art event, Art Fair Tokyo features over 180 galleries exhibiting in the Tokyo International Forum (3-5-1, Marunouchi, Chiyoda). Anime Japan, located in the Tokyo International Exhibition Centre (3-11-3, Ariake, Koto-ku) shows anime-related music, talks, exhibitions and seminars perfect for devoted fans. To make the most of the city's diverse cultural scene, balance out visits to commercial gatherings with smaller independent shows for a well rounded experience.

Masaaki Hiromura
Founder, Hiromura Design Office

Art director and graphic designer born in Aichi in 1954. Portofilo includes graphics and signage design for Miraikan, Yokosuka Museum of Art, 9h Kyoto Teramachi, and Loft Yurakucho.

**21_21 DESIGN SIGHT
P.032**

UltraSuper-New Gallery P.034

Mike Sheetal
Co-founder, UltraSuperNew

Artist, creator and director of creative agency UltraSuper-New. Originally from Australia, he has worked and lived in Japan since 2002. He leads the creative and digital teams at USN.

Miki Moriyama
Design director, Landor Japan

I design mainly for consumer branding. I like movies, books, music, travel, new things, old things, Tokyo and the country. I also like design!

**SCAI THE BATHHOUSE
P.035**

Yo Shitara
CEO, BEAMS Co.,Ltd.

Yo Shitara is the CEO of BEAMS specialty stores. He is a fashion trendsetter in both art and culture. He positions himself as a producer.

**TOKYO CULTUART by BEAMS
P.036**

VACANT P.038

Shuta Hasunuma
Composer & artist

Born in Tokyo in 1983, Shuta Hasunuma produces music with his band Shuta Hasunuma Philharmonic Orchestra. Hasunuma has hosted concerts inside and outside Japan.

Yuki Matsueda
Artist

I transform pictograms into volume and some call me "3D art creator." Happiness and joyfulness is the motto of my life, and the beginning of art.

**Tokyo Metropolitan Museum of Photography
P.039**

Yutaka Maeda
Founder, ujidesign

Art director and comic-lover who owns thousands of manga in the office. I love listening to music and am also interested in politics.

Miraikan
P.041

Kazuhiko Yoshizaki
Curator, MOT

Born in 1980, Kazuhiko Yoshizaki planned shows for the Museum of Contemporary Art Tokyo. He also co-curated "Berlin 2000-2011" in 2011, and the "Francis Alÿs" exhibition in 2012.

Torafu Architects
Architectural firm

Founded by Koichi Suzuno and Shinya Kamuro in 2004. Torafu's work ranges from architecture to interiors, film making, spatial installations and product design.

NHK Studio Park
P.040

Art Center Ongoing
P.044

Nobuo Araki
Founder, The Archetype

Nobuo Araki is an architect. He handles many collaborative projects with creators and artists in Japan and overseas besides designing for housing, offices and galleries.

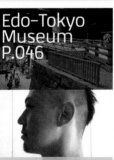

Edo-Tokyo Museum
P.046

Yumiko Chiba
Gallerist & curator

Founded Yumiko Chiba Associates in 1998 for artist management and art planning. Yumiko Chiba opened Yumiko Chiba Associates viewing room in Shinjuku in 2010.

Haruki Sasaki
Designer, FRAPBOIS & ikurah

A graduate from Bunka Fashion College. Haruki Sasaki has worked with TSUMORI CHISATO as assistant designer before inducted into FRAPBOIS in 2005.

Kaikai Kiki Gallery
P.045

Tokyo National Museum
P.047

13 21_21 DESIGN SIGHT
Map D, P.104

Conceptual exhibitions planned by directors
Issey Miyake, Taku Satoh, Naoto Fukasawa,
design journalist Noriko Kawakami and other
design icons re-interpret daily life, from choco-
late to a grain of rice at 21_21 DESIGN SIGHT, one
of Japan's most significant design-focused
spaces. Unique approaches, performances
and talks challenge the well-trotted museum
format, and are held in a Tadao Ando-designed
space inspired by Issey Miyakye's vision of
clothing as "a piece of cloth." Programmes
rotate approximately three times a year.

🕐 1100–2000 (W–M & P.H.)
💲 ¥1,000/800/500
🏠 9-7-6, Akasaka, Minato-ku
📞 +81 (0)3 34 75 21 21
🔗 www.2121designsight.jp

"This is the place where you can see the forefront
of design."
– Masaaki Hiromura, Hiromura Design Office

14 UltraSuperNew Gallery
Map A, P.103

Part concept store part gallery space, this quiet nook is a new venture by creative agency, UltraSuperNew. In operation since September 2013, top curators and artists from Japan and abroad enliven the space located in Tokyo's youth central, with cutting-edge programmes featuring bold images, curious objects and futuristic jewellery, often put up for sale. The gallery is about a 10-minute walk from JR Harajuku. Take Takeshita street, turn left on Meiji street and walk until you see the gallery.

🕙 1000-1900 (M-F), 1300-1800 (Sa)
🏠 1-1-3, Jingumae, Shibuya-ku
📞 +81 (0)3 64 32 93 50
URL ultrasupernew.com/gallery

"It's a gallery I created along with my team and we are very proud of it."
– Mike Sheetal, UltraSuperNew

15 SCAI THE BATHHOUSE

Map J, P.108

Representing names like Tatsuo Miyajima, Mariko Mori, Anish Kapoor and Julian Opie, SCAI is a visual treat. Located in Yanaka's olde-world neighbourhood, the transformed *sento* bathhouse retains its original exterior, tiled roof and boiler. Inside, the white interior shell displays contemporary expressions that blur cultures and artistic disciplines. The gallery has a strong track record of large-scale exhibitions and urban art projects. Among them, Louise Bourgeois' spider-like bronze sculpture, *Maman* (2002), a well-known landmark now found at Roppongi Hills.

🕐 1200-1800 (Tu-Sa except P.H. and between exhibitions)
🏠 6-1-23, Yanaka, Taito-ku   📞 +81 (0)3 38 21 11 44
🔗 www.scaithebathhouse.com

"It's an elegant area surrounded by Nezu and Yanaka. Enjoy a walk in the streets. Ueno Park is close at hand where you can find more museums and galleries."

– Miki Moriyama, Landor Japan

16 TOKYO CULTUART by BEAMS
Map A, P.103

An assortment of unique and collectable art,
gadgets, books and figurines are displayed in
this eccentric third-floor space that looks like a
fusion between an office, museum and lifesize
toy box. Established in Harajuku, clothing brand
BEAMS has managed to showcase the essence
of Tokyo's chaotic and daring design culture,
attracting fashion conscious urbanites who'll
shell out $150 on stuffed figures or rush to
see Pucci's new high fashion furniture range.
TOKYO CULTUART also stages exhibitions and
performances so keep an eye out for updates
on their website.

🕐 1100–2000 (F–W)
🏠 3F–3–24–7, Jingumae, Shibuya-ku
📞 +81 (0)3 34 70 32 51
ⓕ TOKYO CULTUART by BEAMS

*"It is a space where you can enjoy diversified current
culture in Tokyo. Come back whenever you can as we
update events frequently."*
– Yo Shitara, BEAMS Co.,Ltd.

17 VACANT

Map A, P.103

On a quiet backstreet in Harajuku's otherwise teeming teen hotspot, this two-storey space is often referred to as a hub for creative innovation. Operating as an independent gallery, shop and events space, VACANT embraces underground artists, new art and design books and quirky souvenirs. Since opening in May 2009, the site has staged book fairs, flea markets, and live music performances. Sip some expertly-made brews at New Coffee Steppers run by Little Nap COFFEE STAND (#44), while you check out the free Wi-Fi.

🕐 1200-2000 (Tu-Su)
🏠 3-20-13, Jingumae, Shibuya-ku
📞 +81 (0)3 64 59 29 62
URL www.vacant.vc

"Do not miss the events on the second floor!"

– Shuta Hasunuma

18 Tokyo Metropolitan Museum of Photography

Map F, P.105

This Tokyo gem is a museum known for its professional shows and hefty collection of approximately 30,000 photographs and visual media items, including highbrow art pieces, portraits and news pictures. Exhibitions on themes ranging from pure aesthetics to city history rotate periodically over three gallery floors. Take Sky Walk from JR Ebisu's east gate, or the underpass on rainy days to access the museum. Check out annual Yebisu International Festival if travelling in February.

🕐 1000-1800 (Tu–Su & P.H. except Tuesdays after P.H. Mondays), –2000 (Th–F) 💲 Admission varies with programmes 🏠 1-13-3, Mita, Meguro-ku 📞 +81 (0)3 32 80 00 99 🔗 www.syabi.com

"Yebisu is not only about beer. Here, you can admire the works of contemporary photographers."

– Yuki Matsueda

19 NHK Studio Park

Map A, P.102

Curious kids and grown-ups will revel in this opportunity to learn about Japan's famous public broadcaster. Fresh from a complete overhaul headed by ujidesign in 2011, NHK Studio Park presents latest broadcasting technologies, interactive exhibits and production studios, where you can dub in your voice along to animations or partake in news programme production (by appointment only). The park offers a shuttle bus service from Shibuya station (outside Shibuya Mark City).

🕐 1000–1800 daily (except monthly 4th Mondays or Tuesdays after P.H. 4th Mondays) 💲 ¥200/-
🏠 2-2-1, Jinnan, Shibuya-ku
📞 +81 (0)3 34 85 80 34
🔗 www.nhk.or.jp/studiopark

"NHK is the most famous TV station in Japan and the theme park has been fully renewed. Pay a very small fee and you can spend a day here."

– Yutaka Maeda, ujidesign

20 Miraikan
Map O, P.109

Hands-on displays, robots, gadgets and high-tech multimedia presentations at *Miraikan* (Hall of the Future) are fuel for curious minds. Properly known as the National Museum of Emerging Science and Innovation, the facility drafts expertise from top scientists, engineers, artists and architects to decode life science, the universe and information. Highlights include a 3D theatre with shows explaining the universe's birth, Honda robot ASIMO and a giant glowing Geo-Cosmos globe displaying up-to-the-minute data on climate conditions and wildlife movements occurring around the world.

🕙 1000-1700 (W-M)　💲 ¥620/210
🏠 2-3-6, Aomi, Koto-ku　📞 +81 (0)3 35 70 91 88
🔗 www.miraikan.jst.go.jp/en

"Enjoy the world of 'spatial information science' and 'Song of Anagura' we created. Floor-to-ceiling projections turn the room into a huge game space."

– Torafu Architects

21 Art Center Ongoing
Map N, P.109

The concept "Ongoing" originated as a regular meeting point for a group of 70s-born artists to share creation without limitation. The notion to foster an appreciation for new art gradually developed into this percolating alternative hub, with a cross-disciplinary programme of artist and curatorial residencies, and exhibitions featuring diverse subjects that change every two weeks. Read art books over good homemade meals, or attend public forums and live shows held every weekend at the ground-floor café.

🕐 1200–2300 (W–Su), Gallery: –2100 🆂 ¥400 🏠 1-8-7, Kichijoji Higashicho, Musashino-shi
📞 +81 (0)4 22 26 84 54
URL www.ongoing.jp

"Discover Japanese young talent whenever you visit here. They often meet together at the café on the ground floor."

– Kazuhiko Yoshizaki, MOT

22 Kaikai Kiki Gallery
Map D, P.104

Art installations, photography and paintings from local and international figures turn this basement gallery into an unmistakable beacon of art. World-respected contemporary artist and founder Takashi Murakami personally curates the shows, and includes his most recent projects. He also runs Kaikai Kiki Co., representing 'superflat' artists like Chiho Aoshima and Aya Takano, also displayed. Be sure to check out art-fuelled Bar Zingaro in Nakano Broadway (#33), Murakami's Scandinavian-themed bar, the artist's first step into food and drink.

🕐 1100-1900 (Tu-Sa, except P.H. & in between exhibitions) 🏠 Motoazabu Crest Bldg., B1F-2-3-30, Motoazabu, Minato-ku 📞 +81 (0)3 68 23 60 38
🔗 en.gallery-kaikaikiki.com

"It is a unique gallery with tatami floor. The owner, Takashi Murakami, is one of my favourite artists."

– Nobuo Araki, The Archetype

23 **Edo-Tokyo Museum**
Map Q, P.110

1868's renaming of the city from Edo to Tokyo marked the end of the country's feudal era and the dawn of modern Japan. Edo power and strength are represented in scenes that recur frequently as *ukiyoe* (portrayals of the fleeting world) at Edo-Tokyo Museum, modelled on an archaic warehouse. In separate zones, faithful replicas detail the city's history from Edo to the 1960s when rapid economic growth began. The adjacent Sumo Museum and Stadium is dedicated to the longstanding national sport.

🕐 0930-1730 (Tu-Su & P.H. except Tuesdays after P.H. Mondays), -1930 (Sa) 💲 ¥600/480/300
🏠 1-4-1, Yokoami, Sumida-ku 📞 +81 (0)3 36 26 99 74
🔗 www.edo-tokyo-museum.or.jp
🔗 Separate admission for special exhibitions

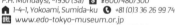

"Their exhibition is worth seeing. Real-to-life settings will transport you to the Edo era. Foreign visitors will be amazed!"

– Haruki Sasaki, FRAPBOIS & ikurah

24 Tokyo National Museum

Map J, P.108

Arguably the oldest national art museum in Japan, Tokyo National Museum, inside Ueno Park, offers a fine view of Japanese and Asian culture stretching back into prehistory. Four exhibition buildings each feature a distinctive focus, with *Honkan* (Main Gallery) exhibiting Japanese art, *Heiseikan* showing ancient artifacts, Yoshio Taniguchi-designed gallery displaying Horyuji Treasures and *Toyokan* showing Asian art. Ueno Park is also home to a few other museums, a zoo and is a popular spot for cherry viewing in spring.

🕒 *0930-1700 (Tu-Su & P.H. except Tuesdays after P.H. Mondays)* 💲 *¥620/410* 🏠 *13-9, Uenokoen, Taito-ku* 📞 *+81 (0)3 54 05 86 86* 🔗 *www.tnm.jp*

"Just pay a small price and you can travel through cultures from the Jomon era to modern time."

– Yumiko Chiba

Markets & Shops

Designer labels, clever housewares and Japanese delicacies

Shops in this city cater to every niche and demand imaginable. From high fashion brands to shops offering over 200 varieties of clothes hangers, anything goes here in retail. Luckily, there are specific hotspots where certain goods are sold so that efficient shopping can be planned. Harajuku is a must-see destination for the fashion curious and a stroll through this area will tempt anyone with a camera. Dwellers in this unofficial capital of youth culture take their clothing very seriously, creating head turning outfits. Ikebukuro is home to some of the largest department stores and electronic chains, and happens to be a short walk from Japan's second busiest train station – Ikebukuro station. For the trademark anime and manga that Tokyo is known for, visit Akihabara for a plethora of shops solely dedicated to collectibles, games and figurines. Often, an unplanned journey to one of the city's quieter areas unearths independent retailers – a wander down Shimokitazawa reveals some great vintage at wonderfully cheap prices. Whilst Ameyoko-cho Market (4, *Ueno, Taito-ku*), one of Tokyo's oldest market streets, presents a range of food and souvenir shops and is a short distance from Ueno Zoo.

Takashi Kato
Design journalist

Born in Tokyo. I publish my views and writings on architecture, design and art on my blog 'FORM_Story of design.'

THE SHOP
P.053

Manabu Mizuno
Founder, good design company

My work spans from corporate branding to consultancy, recognised by the Gold Pencil at One Show Design and Big 3 Advertising Awards inside and outside Japan.

Akiko Kanna
Art director, StudioKanna

Tokyo-based graphic design studio StudioKanna specialises in corporate identity and print design.

classico
P.052

TAKEO
MIHONCHO
HONTEN
P.054

Satoshi Itasaka
Architect, h220430

I established "h220430" to create products, lighting and furniture. We want to design not just the primary shape of things but also communication derived from the messages in things.

Sakata
P.057

Daisuke Motogi
Architect

I'm born in 1981 in Kumagaya, Saitama and am a 2004 graduate from Musashino Art University. I worked at Schemata Architecture Office before I started Daisuke Motogi Architecture in 2010.

Noritaka Tatehana
Fashion designer

With a background in fine arts, sculpture, dyeing and weaving, I make *getas* (Japanese clogs) using traditional Japanese dyeing method, *Yuzen*. I established my own *maison*, NORITAKA TATEHANA in 2010.

HIGASHIYA
GINZA
P.056

TRADING
MUSEUM
COMME des
GARÇONS
P.058

Junsuke Yamasaki
Fashion editor & publisher

Born and raised in Tokyo, I started my own zine project *untitled* in 2010 and was an editor at *VOGUE HOMME JAPAN* until 2012. I trained as classical ballet dancer and am teaching dance with an old friend.

CHRISTOPHER NEMETH P.060

Furuhonyugi Ruroudo P.061

Hiroshi Eguchi
Founder, UTRECHT

Representative of 'UTRECHT,' a book shop in Omotesando and director of 'THE TOKYO ART BOOK FAIR.' I love udon noodles!

Shinichiro Kitai
Art director, DEVILROBOTS

DEVILROBOTS is a five-man design team established in 1997. Focus includes graphic design, character design, illustration, web designs, and project planning for clients from Japan, Asia and beyond.

Nakano Broadway P.062

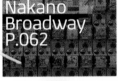

Yasuhiko Fukuzono
Co-founder, flau

I'm the owner of record label 'flau,' DJ, joker and producer. I also produce music under moniker 'aus.'

Disk Union Shinjuku Main Store P.063

Farmer's Market at UNU P.064

Atsushi Umezawa
Founder, Glam Beast

Art director and graphic designer who has spent three years in the UK before moving back to Tokyo and founding Glam Beast. I art direct fashion ads, CD covers, and teach.

Koshi Kawachi
Artist

A Tokyo-based artist active inside and outside Japan. My notable works include "Tasty Buddha" carved from Umaibo, and "Manga Farming" where radish sprouts are grown between book pages.

Togoshi Ginza Shotengai P.065

25 classico

Map J, P.108

As the name suggests, every item at quaint retail space Classico embraces a clean and classic aesthetic. Realised in downtown Yanaka in 2006, the store has since drawn a committed crowd attracted to its minimalist clothing collections, unfussy home supplies and quirky antiques. Owner Takahashi-*san*, puts to good use impeccable taste and two decades of fashion industry experience to select every item displayed. Browse delicate ceramics created by local artisans or refine your stationery collection with sleek notebooks and pens.

🕐 1200-1900 (W-M)
🏠 2-5-22-102, Yanaka, Taito-ku
📞 +81 (0)3 38 23 76 22
URL www.classico-life.com

"Enjoy a walk around the classic Tokyo neighbourhood and stop by the Nezu shrine - it's one of our traditional Japanese icons."

– Takashi Kato

26 THE SHOP
Map I, P.107

Curated and managed by product designer Keita Suzuki of Product Design Centre, Jun Nakagawa of craft business Nakagawa Masashichi Shoten Co. Ltd., and Manabu Mizuno of good design company, THE SHOP's founders scout the world for cleverly crafted home goods, stationery, and clothing that are often environmentally aware. The owners regularly work on and showcase collaborations that refine daily essentials and like to highlight goods with a vivid brand story.

🕐 1100–2100 (M–Sa & day before P.H.), –2000 (Su & P.H.)
🏠 KITTE, 4F–2–7–2, Marunouchi, Chiyoda–ku
📞 +81 (0)3 32 17 20 08 URL the-web.co.jp

"You will find great things for your own home or friends."
– Manabu Mizuno, good design company

27 **TAKEO MIHONCHO HONTEN**
Map K, P.108

As a leader of paper development processes since 1899, TAKEO represents around 300 paper brands and trades about 2,700 items including fine papers with innovative patterns or texture. At this showroom and shop, visitors can learn everything about papers, printing and processing, from papers made with timeworn traditional techniques to new, cutting-edge technology. Compare papers by colour gradients on the first floor and read references on paper design upstairs. Check dates for the annual exhibition, TAKEO PAPER SHOW, which displays paper products based around a theme.

🕐 1000–1900 (M–F except P.H.)
🏠 3-18-3, Kandanishikicho, Chiyoda-ku
📞 +81 (0)3 32 92 36 69
🔗 www.takeo.co.jp

"Simply write down the codes of the papers if you want to purchase and their staff will pick up the papers for you."

– Akiko Kanna, StudioKanna

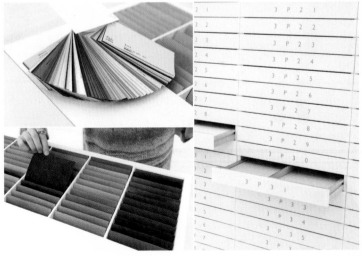

28 **HIGASHIYA GINZA**
Map I, P.107

Head to Higashiya Ginza to try Japan's unique *wagashi*, or traditional confectionary. The shop offers an appetising selection of sweets most usually to be eaten paired with tea. Try sweet *mochi* rice cakes, light sponge cakes and bean-paste desserts, all beautifully packaged. Also stocked on shelves are collections of specialty tea ware. If you'd like to try the products on the spot, head to the tea salon at the back of the shop. Afternoon tea sets are served 2–5pm, or until 6pm on Sundays and public holidays.

🕐 1100–1900 (Tu-Su & P.H. except Tuesdays after P.H. Mondays)
🏠 POLA Ginza bldg., 2F-1-7-7, Ginza, Chuo-ku
📞 +81 (0)3 35 38 32 30 🔗 www.higashiya.com
🔗 Tea salon: –2200 (Tu-Sa)

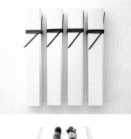

"You must try matcha (Japanese green tea for tea ceremony) and wagashi."

– Satoshi Itasaka, h220430

29 Sakata
Map H, P.106

Sakata is what you might call Tokyo's best known secret. Established over 40 years ago, owner Kazumi Sakata handpicks each and every item for the store, with impressive clients such as late essayist Masako Shirasu championing the dealer's unrivalled taste and knowledge. However, don't expect objects of extreme monetary value – charm and uniqueness are prioritised here. Seemingly unassuming finds include retro swimming goggles from the Showa period or vintage Swatch and Mandaine watches.

🕐 *Flexible opening hours (Tu–Su)*
🏠 *3-18-9, Shimoochiai, Shinjuku-ku*
📞 *+81 (0)3 39 53 63 12*
🔗 *sakatakazumi.com*

"Lose yourself in their excellent selections of refined aesthetic insights."

– Daisuke Motogi

30 TRADING MUSEUM COMME des GARÇONS

Map A, P.103

A retail space created to exist beyond trends and outside fashion, where barriers between trading and museum spaces come tumbling down. Envisioned by fashion hard hitter Rei Kawakubo, founder of Comme des Garçons, the select edits and collections carries the museum's spirit to engage, educate and provoke. Grab the opportunity to view rare and one-off items by sought-after and emergent designers alongside some of the pieces that propelled the Japanese fashion house into the global limelight. And don't feel pressured to buy. "Just looking" is welcomed in this space, where shopping is not encouraged as the sole aim.

🕐 1100–2000 daily
🏠 Gyre, 2F–5–10–1, Jingumae, Shibuya-ku
📞 +81 (0)3 34 86 85 90

"Most things you can find here are exclusive to this shop, so please find your one and only treasure. You can find my shoes here too."

– Noritaka Tatehana

31 CHRISTOPHER NEMETH
Map A, P.103

Tokyo-based British artist and fashion designer Christopher Nemeth (1959-2010) is known for his dishevelled garments that display a raw, daring and individual feel. Having harboured frustration at not finding clothing he liked, Nemeth initially created his own by hand-sewing old fabrics and material remnants shortly after he graduated art school in 1982. Still a mainstay in the street fashion circuit, trendsetters have embraced his work since he arrived to Tokyo in 1986. His flagship store in Omotesando remains the go-to place for his unique pieces.

🕐 1400-2000 daily
🏠 4-13-5, Jingumae, Shibuya-ku
☎ +81 (0)3 34 01 21 23
URL www.christophernemeth.co

"If you are looking for something underground, Christopher's 'handmade' store is full of his treasures."
– Junsuke Yamasaki

32 Furuhonyugi Ruroudou
Map B, P.103

Rare is the occasion these days that clever initiatives do not show up on the Internet radar, but Furuhonyugi Ruroudou is one such place. The extensive secondhand bookshop is nestled just across the street from the long-established cake shop MATTERHORN near Gakugeidaigaku station. No amount of 'Googling' will reveal the exact selection on offer, so be prepared for a truly explorative browse. One thing is guaranteed though – you are assured to find a bargain or two among a trove of artsier publications.

🕐 1200-0000 (M-Sa, except monthly 2nd & 4th Tuesdays), 1100-2300 (Su & P.H.) 🏠 3-6-9-103, Takaban, Meguro-ku 📞 +81 (0)3 37 92 30 82

> "See the world through the art books, picture books, and old posters that cover the wall and the ceiling, enhanced by the owner's taste and span of time."
>
> – Hiroshi Eguchi, UTRECHT

33 Nakano Broadway
Map G, P.106

A short walk from Nakano station, this four-storey shopping complex offers an unrivalled experience of Japanese pop culture. First wander around the ground floor for clothing, shoes and vintage stores before venturing to the second and third floor to explore an anime and manga paradise where shoppers can find character figures, costumes, video games, playing cards and other souvenirs. Visit the Mandarake stores for anime collectables and grab an oversized ice cream from Tokudai Soft Creams for $4.

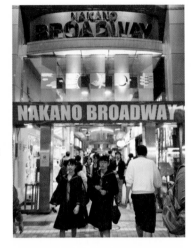

🕙 *Opening hours vary with shops*
🏠 *5-52-15, Nakano, Nakano-ku*
📞 *+81 (0)3 33 88 70 04*
🔗 *www.nbw.jp*

"Toys Toys Toys!"

– Shinichiro Kitai, DEVILROBOTS

34 Disk Union Shinjuku Main Store

Map E, P.105

Music lovers of all stripes will rejoice in Disk Union's miles of musical wares. Draw up a wishlist and start by visiting its main store on Higashiguchi Chuo street. Eight floors of music supply mostly new and used rock and indie records, with Latin and Brazilian on the fourth floor. Follow drawings by comic artists Takashi Nemoto and Gataro Man to find exclusive labels and underground Japanese rock bands in the basement. Should you desire more, Disk Union also has a jazz store on the same street, and ten other specialised outlets for heavy metal, punk, dance, blues, and classical all in the same area.

🕘 1100–2100 (M–Sa), –2000 (Su & P.H.) 🏠 Yamada bldg., 3-31-4, Shinjuku, Shinjuku-ku 📞 +81 (0)3 33 52 26 91 🔗 diskunion.net

"*It has a very big secondhand record shop where you can find rare LP/CD and meet music geeks.*"

– Yasuhiko Fukuzono, flau

35 Farmer's Market at UNU

Map A, P.103

Every weekend some 60 organic smallholders, flower farmers and beekeepers from all over country gather in front of United Nation University vending regional specialties. Mountains of fruits, vegetables, herbs, teas and honey converge with food carts that rustle up delicacies using only organic and pesticide-free ingredients. Take your chance to sample Japanese fresh produce, then head over to Aoyama Book Center's main store at Cosmos Aoyama Garden (behind the academy) for local design books and magazines.

🕙 1000-1600 (Sa-Su)
🏠 5-53-70, Jingumae, Shibuya-ku
URL www.farmersmarkets.jp

"There is no veggie market in Tokyo like this one. Early bird catches the worm."

– Atsushi Umezawa, Glam Beast

36 Togoshi Ginza Shotengai
Map P, P.110

A local crowd stroll along this street nightly, which at 1.3km, is one of Japan's longest shopping strips. Over 400 shops inject heapfulls of character, with supermarkets, barbershops, butchers and *pachinkos* (local casinos) jostling both sides of the street. Divided into shopping districts – Shoeikai, Chuogai and Ginrokukai – the shopping boasts myriad small independents. Look out for charming little food shops often run by elderly owners selling goods from the storefronts.

🏠 Yutakacho, Togoshi & Hiratsuka, Shinagawa-ku
URL www.togoshiginza.jp

"Experience the real everyday life of Tokyo residents here!"
– Koshi Kawachi

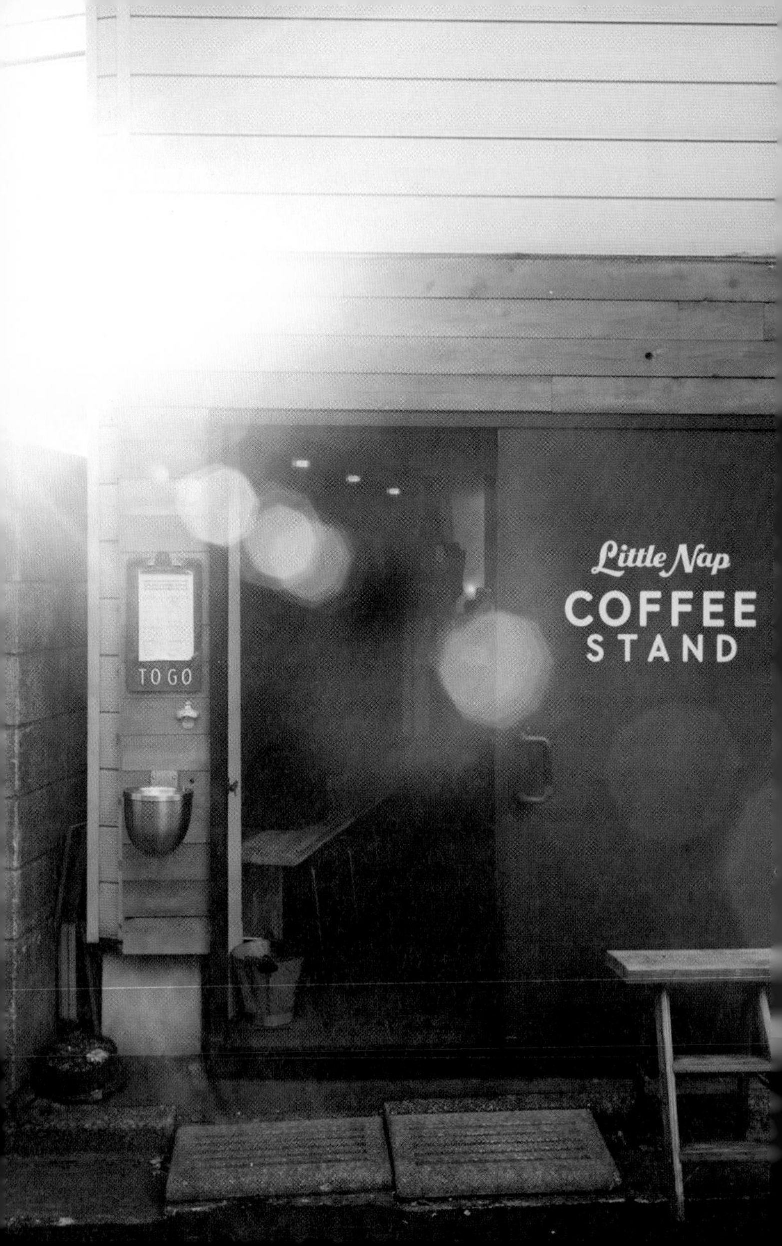
TOGO
Little Nap
COFFEE
STAND

Restaurants & Cafés

Deluxe kaiseki, unrivalled street food and expert coffee

Japanese take their cuisine very seriously and as a result, the region has some of the most revered restaurants in the world. Food outlets combine carefully curated ingredients with a delicate presentation style that marries perfectly Tokyo's innovative culture. Specialities differ from region to region but you'll find that restaurants usually focus on a specific cooking style or component, ensuring high quality and precision. *Teppanyaki* refers to outlets that resemble steakhouses whilst *robatayaki* restaurants offer seafood and meats cooked on an open charcoal grill. For a more sophisticated night out, try out *kaiseki* cuisine. Aesthetic appeal and delicate arrangement characterise this more expensive range of dishes hand-selected by the chef.

Etiquette in Japan is especially important so it's advisable to study the basics before starting any culinary adventures. Eating and drinking on the move is largely considered ill mannered, with the exception of festivals, so try to finish your snacks near the vendor before venturing off.

A great way to impress locals is to freshen up your chopstick skills. Feel free to lift bowls or plates closer to the mouth when eating, but remember to never point your chopsticks towards others. If you're finding it difficult, ask a Japanese person to show you.

Kotaro Watanabe
Creative director

A design engineer, author and entrepreneur spliting time between Athens, Hong Kong and Brussels. I endeavour to integrate poetry and technology at the firm, takram design engineering.

Seijo
9-Chome
Cafe
P.070

SODO
P.071

Daijiro Ohara
Art director, OMOMMA™

I'm born in 1978 and schooled at Musashino Art University. My design practice OMOMMA™ focuses on art direction, handmade graphics, typography, illustrations and animation.

Claudio Colucci
Designer

A designer from Switzerland, working between interior and product design. My creative bases are Tokyo, Paris, Shanghai, and Geneva.

Sahsya
Kanetanaka
P.072

Harubarutei
P.074

so+ba
Multidisciplinary design studio

Originally from Switzerland, Alex (so)nderegger and Susanna (ba)er started so+ba in Tokyo in 2001. so+ba also teaches typography and design at Tama Art University.

Morihiro Harano
Creative director, Mori Inc.

Harano is an all-rounder with achievements in advertising, media initiatives and product design. He co-founded PARTY and founded Mori Inc. in 2012.

Tokyo Shiba
Tofuya-Ukai
P.073

Toru Muto
Sales promoter, AMBIDEX

A member of apparel company AMBIDEX's sales promotion team. My work centres around sales, including promotion, interior design and events for AMBIDEX and its branches.

Cafe Grill
Bar Taiyo
P.075

Mari Katayama
Artist & fashion model

Born in 1987, Katayama has both legs amputated at nine and made her own self portraits with prosthetic legs. She is now also a musician, a fashion model and a lecturer involved in diverse fields.

TRAUMARIS
P.076

Little Nap
COFFEE
STAND
P.077

Nendesign inc.
Creative agency

A creative team back in London, Yoshihiro Yoshida and Shiho Kikuchi established Nendesign in Japan in 2009. Creative focuses include brand identity and development, art direction, and interactive design.

Yu Yamada
President, method inc.

Creative director of method inc., independent curator, and also a buyer working for an array of retailers mainly in Japan.

(marunouchi)
HOUSE
P.078

Tomohiko Yoneda
Editor & writer, Nomad Tokyo

I started Nomad Tokyo in 2011, travelling and living across Tokyo using Social Networking Service (SNS), without home or office. My journey is condensed into a book, called "*Life Style Design In Our Age (JP).*"

Harmonica
Yokocho
P.081

Yuki Udagawa
Creative director & PR, BAUM

I create solutions for social issues, working in partnership with national clients, NPO's, NGO's and government.

Naoki Ga
Creative director, W+K Tokyo

Born and grew up in Tokyo, lived and worked in New York and Singapore in the past and been with W+K Tokyo for over seven years.

Innsyoutei
P.080

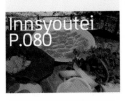

Robot
Restaurant
P.082

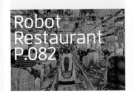

37 Seijo 9-Chome Cafe
Map R, P.111

Strangers might be unexpected but they are still most welcome at this modest local café lodged in a quiet residential area, named after Seijo University and flanked by two winding subsidiaries of the Tama River. Gallery space and dining area integrates, and bountiful pot plants and antiquities quickly turn this tiny glassed-in lodge into a perfect place for meeting friends or whiling away the hours. Find a seat between the little art pieces – handmade by the owner herself – then tuck into wholesome dishes prepared daily in-house.

🕐 1100-1800 (Tu-Sa)
🏠 9-15-5, Seijo, Setagaya-ku
📞 +81 (0)3 34 82 79 75
URL www.seijo9.com

"Go for a hearty daily special lunch and coffee, brewed using 9-Chome's own blend!"
– Kotaro Watanabe, takram design engineering

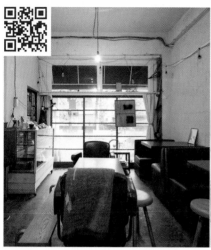

38 SODO

Star percussionist and owner Yosuke Hosokubo's love for tunes, living and hot brews is unassumingly woven into the details of this mellow little café and *zakka*-store near Kamimachi station (Tokyu Setagaya line). Good music and the wonderful aroma of fresh made coffee and on-site bakery mingle in this cultured enclave, with sleek furniture and original utensils from Hosokubo's 'happy lifestyle' Blue Beat Project. SODO also hosts music shows, exhibitions by local artists and Sunday markets during warm weather seasons. Tea addicts should sample SODO's special blends.

☎ +81 (0)3 34 28 80 07
URL sodo-coffee.jimdo.com

"Their coffee is so tasty!"
– Daijiro Ohara, OMOMMA™

39 Sahsya Kanetanaka
Map A, P.103

Kanetanaka restaurants are famous for their fine *kaiseki* (traditional multi-course meals) and desserts that are finished with tastes of the season. The experience is elevated at their latest outpost, found inside commercial complex oak omotesando, with artist Hiroshi Sugimoto's sensational work charging the decor. Reclaim peace amidst the bustling Omotesando avenue at this sanctuary-like venue where Sugimoto handpicked the massive stones and installed a sculpture honouring mathematical precision over the entryway, which is visible from the private dining room.

🕙 1130–2030 daily 🏠 oak omotesando, 2F-3-6-1, Kitaaoyama, Minato-ku 📞 +81 (0)3 64 50 51 16
URL www.kanetanaka.co.jp/restrant/sahsya/index.html

"Review Hiroshi Sugimoto's work to comtemplate the details of its interior space."

– Claudio Colucci

40 Tokyo Shiba Tofuya-Ukai
Map I, P.106

Taking pride in their fresh made tofu, Tokyo Shiba Tofuya-Ukai dishes out traditional *kaiseki* that pleases the pickiest gourmet. Specialty bean curd is artfully crafted daily with the finest locally sourced soybeans, spring water and natural (bittern) salt that matches seasonal fish, sashimi, grills, stewed meat and vegetables next to a 6,000sqm private garden and the iconic TOKYO TOWER (#1). Request a private room with pure tatami flooring if you come in a group.

🕐 1100-2200 daily
🏠 4-4-13, Shibakoen, Minato-ku
📞 +81 (0)3 34 36 10 28
URL www.ukai.co.jp/english/shiba

"Dinner is recommended. Make reservation three months in advance."

– Morihiro Harano, Mori Inc.

41 Harubarutei
Map S, P.111

Just a two-minute walk away from Kyodo station, this quaint, hospitable ramen place fills hungry stomachs with delightful recipes and specialty drinks. With only eight seats lining the front of the kitchen, the shop fills out quickly with regulars returning for the appetising noodle selection, served in soup or dry. Add the house black vinegar and home-style chilli paste for a refreshing taste. Harubarutei usually takes a summer vacation and closes, especially in August.

 1200–1500, 1700–2030 (Th–M)
2-15-15, Kyodo, Setagaya-ku
+81 (0)3 34 27 32 42

"This is the best ramen store in Tokyo. Try their original drinks. Our favourite is 'Anarchy' and 'Egon Schiele.'"

– so+ba

42 Cafe Grill Bar Taiyo

Map L, P.109

Even the distant sound of cars on the nearby national highway doesn't disturb the laid-back vibe at this spot, where esteemed designer and typographic artist Fumio Tachibana took a hand in the interior design. Reasonably-priced lunch sets are tasty, or try the classic menu for two. Balanced plates with fish or meat, vegetable, curry and snacks are prepared with home-cooked flare. Smoking is allowed indoors.

🕐 1130–1600, 1900–0100 (M–F), 1830–0100 (Sa)
🏠 1-3-6, Ohashi, Meguro-ku
📞 +81 (0)3 37 80 09 44 URL taiyoo.exblog.jp

"The atmosphere will take the stress off your shoulders and let you enjoy their delicious food."

– Toru Muto, AMBIDEX

43 TRAUMARIS
Map F, P.105

TRAUMARIS is a charming little artist den hidden away above art-filled NADiff a/p/a/r/t building in Ebisu. With four galleries and a bar housed in the building, workshops and exhibitions on literature, music, film, dance and design summon an art-loving crowd who also seeks out its hearty food prepared from family recipes. Get there before sunset to scour the entire building for great art objects and books.

🕐 1600–0000 (Tu–Sa), 1400–2200 (Su)
🏠 NADiff a/p/a/r/t, 3F-1-18-4, Ebisu, Shibuya-ku 📞 +81 (0)3 64 08 55 22
🌐 www.traumaris.jp

"The owner, Chie Sumiyoshi, is also an art-writer. Exhibitions curated with her foresight are overwhelming!!!"

– Mari Katayama

 44 **Little Nap COFFEE STAND**
Map A, P.102

Hidden away on a quiet residential street just a few steps away from Yoyogi Park, it's heavenly to kill some time at this cool little café. A simple menu offers blissful basics – freshly ground coffee and homemade gelato with seasonal flavours, complemented with a large window that lets in the street view. You'll also find a handful of organic goods, bags and shirts on site.

🕐 0900–1900 (Tu-Su)
🏠 5-65-4, Yoyogi, Shibuya-ku
📞 +81 (0)3 34 66 00 74
URL www.littlenap.jp

"It's a creative people's favourite hangout. Of course they serve great coffee."

– Nendesign inc.

45 (marunouchi) HOUSE
Map I, P.107

Console yourself here if you miss the last train home! Fashionable bars and hip restaurants overflow to cover the entire seventh floor of Shinmarubiru. Tease your tastebuds until 4am, on fusion, Japanese tapas, grill specials and steamed-only menus, then drink cocktails or show off your singing talents at the karaoke-geared pub. Don't miss the chance to admire JR Tokyo station, built in 1914, and viewable from the open-air terrace.

🕐 1100–0400 (M-Sa), –2300 (Su & P.H.)
🏠 Shinmarubiru, 7F-1-5-1, Marunouchi, Chiyoda-ku
🔗 www.marunouchi-house.com
🖉 Opening hours vary with shops, Enter via JR Tokyo station from 1100

"The entire floor filled with nice restaurants and bars. It's a high quality food court for adults."

– Yu Yamada, method inc.

46 Innsyoutei
Map J, P.108

Tree-shrouded Innsyoutei has been gratifying visitors to Ueno Park since 1875, and most of its original features are in good repair. Tea and snacks on the ground floor are served within a timber tearoom, with lunch and dinner served in an upstairs dining room – some with tatami. A choice of lunch options includes *bento* or casual *kaiseki*, while for dinner expect more formal *kaiseki* or *sukiyaki* (simmered chicken or beef) prepared by staff while you take in soul-soothing views over the park.

🕐 1100–1500, 1700–2300 daily except end of year & New Year 🏠 4-59, Uenokoen, Taito-ku
📞 +81 (0)3 38 21 81 26 🔗 www.innsyoutei.jp
💳 Cash only

"There's a sense of season in everything they serve. Make a reservation in advance if you go there in cherry blossom season (late March to early April)."

– Tomohiko Yoneda, Nomad Tokyo

47 Harmonica Yokocho
Map N, P.109

Anyone with a yen for street food should stop by Harmonica Yokocho, a lively area of red lanterns, sizzling grills and a tireless crowd located just north of Kichijoji station. About a hundred shops, countertop bars and *izakayas* are crammed into what was once a postwar black market trying to win over peckish shoppers. Nowadays the area attracts white-collars workers and college students looking to feast on *yakitori* (meat skewers) curry and stews. The rush starts from 5pm.

🕐 *Opening hours vary with shops*
🏠 *Kichijojihoncho, Musashino-shi*

"A place where old-fashioned pubs and modern bars co-exist. Some bars have rooftops, enjoy."
– Yuki Udagawa, BAUM

48 **Robot Restaurant**
Map E, P.105

Soak up the Japanese craze for anime in this frenetic Kabukicho hideaway, which bursts flashing neon lights and pulsating beats. The stars of the futuristic show are bikini-clad women sitting astride and battling robots. Drinks are reasonable, and a *bento* box is thrown in with the ticket price, but don't hold out for gourmet fare – the ladies here are definitely the main attraction. Reserve a seat for one of the hour-long shows ahead of time, and confirm your seat on the day.

🕐 *Shows (75mins): 1840, 2020, 2200 (M-F), 1700, 1840, 2020, 2200 (Sa-Su)*
💲 *¥6,000* 🏠 *Shinjuku Robot bldg., B2F-1-7-1, Kabukicho, Shinjuku-ku*
📞 *+81 (0)3 32 00 55 00*
🔢 *www.robot-restaurant.com/E*

"It's hard to explain and I don't want to take the surprise away too much. I'd rather you check it with your own eyes."

– Naoki Ga, W+K Tokyo

Nightlife

Rambunctious raves, artist meet & greets, and after dark views

This high-tech metropolis transforms into a glowing utopia as soon as the sun hits the horizon. Neon lights flag up the staggering variety of dance clubs, gay bars, jazz shows and reggae spots, with entertainments often open till 5am. Unlike many other regions, however, Tokyo doesn't have a nightlife centre, rather, like pockets of gold, they are to be discovered scattered across the city.

Roppongi is popular among foreigners with its swanky offering of upscale bars and dance clubs where socialites let loose and come to mingle. Shibuya is filled with teens and 20-somethings who are up for lighthearted fun within the many mega-clubs and small bars, whilst Shinjuku-ni-chrome is home to over 200 bars open for the gay community. For a truly energetic rave, try out ageHA (*2-2-10, Shinkiba, Koto-ku*), Tokyo's biggest club which boasts crowds of 5000. Feria (*7-13-7, Roppongi, Minato-ku*) is a classy alternative for a chilled out night where luxury drinks and sophisticated music overtakes five floors, and comes with a romantic rooftop view of the city. Alternatively, it would be a shame to miss out on the infamous karaoke nights, where microphone-wielding guests indulge in their favourite classics till dawn.

Tamae Hirokawa
Fashion designer, SOMARTA

I'm also CEO of SOMA DESIGN, a creative firm specialising in fashion, graphic, product, sound design, and short movie. Client list features Toyota, Canon and Lady GAGA.

DAIKANYAMA TSUTAYA BOOKS P.089

Philip Giordano
Illustrator

Italian-born illustrator whose work comes alive in magazine and book covers, children's books, as toys and as animation. You can find my drawings in American illustration annuals and *Monocle*.

Klein Dytham architecture
Architectural firm

Set up by Astrid Klein and Mark Dytham, Klein Dytham is active in architecture and interior design. The Japanese thirst for the new sensitivity to material and detail in crafting nourish KDa's ideas and production.

TWO ROOMS GRILL BAR P.088

SuperDeluxe P.090

New York Bar P.093

Yuko Fukuba
Creative director, DDB

My expertise lies mainly in communication and advertising. Born, raised and based in Tokyo. Pursuing beauty in life, loving good food, good people, nature and smoking cigars.

MIHO
Founder, Saji

I am a photographer and, in 2004, I founded Saji, a concept that has grown from a magazine to include food events, workshops and eating in Tokyo and Paris.

Nobuyuki Hanabusa
Visual artist & director, enra

I create video, motion graphics, illustration, stage art direction and cross-genre. My 2012 collaboration with music band "Bang on a Can" in NY was recognised by the New York Times.

Black List Tokyo P.092

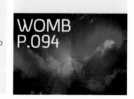

WOMB P.094

Shunya Hagiwara
Web designer

A programmer, a designer, an editor and a planner. My work widely and energetically centres on web design and internet art.

Trick or Treat Horror Dining P.097

TAKAKO
Make-up artist

Beauty specialist. I dedicated myself to bringing the charm of each woman beyond hair styling and make-up.

Keisuke Matsushima
Chef

Born in 1977, I opened "Kei's passion (now KEISUKE MAT-SUSHIMA)" in Nice in 2002, and earned a Michelin star in 2006. I also own "Restaurant-I" in Tokyo and won "L'ORDRE DES ARTS ET DES LETTRES."

Yako P.096

Ebisu Yokocho P.098

Novumichi Tosa
Co-founder, Maywa Denki

Maywa Denki was named after Tosa's father's firm. Together with their work uniform costume, the art unit honours small enterprises that had contributed to Japan's thriving economy during the boom.

LOFT/PLUS ONE P.100

Mitsuo Murai
Editor

Born in Tokyo in 1976, Murai is an editor and founder of Nanarokusha Publishing Co. since 2008. Nanarokusha books feature poem books, photo books and art books available in Japan and overseas.

Shogo Kishino
Founder, 6D

The art director, graphic designer and president of 6D in Minato-ku, Tokyo. My work has been well recognised by awards, like Cannes Lions Design Awards GOLD and D&AD Yellow Pencil.

Vampire P.099

Mahakala P.101

 49 **TWO ROOMS GRILL BAR**
Map A, P.103

Perched on the fifth floor of the iconic AO building in trendy Aoyama, TWO ROOMS is a slick, sensual spot for those after the finer things in life. Over 1800 bottles of select wines from Europe, Australia, New Zealand, South Africa and the Americas are laid out in the entryway, ready to match suave menus of caviar and raw oyster plates, steak sandwiches and homemade ice-creams. The bar also serves a fine selection of beers and specialty drinks.

🕐 Bar: 1130–0200 (M–Sa), –2200 (Su & P.H.), Dinner: 1800–2300 (M–Sa), –2200 (Su & P.H.)
🏠 AO Building, 5F-3-11-7, Kitaaoyama, Minato-ku
📞 +81 (0)3 34 98 00 02 URL www.tworooms.jp
✎ Last order: 1 hour before closing

 "Enjoy the night view of Tokyo with numerous kinds of wine from all over the world."

– Tamae Hirokawa, SOMARTA

50 DAIKANYAMA TSUTAYA BOOKS

Map F P.105

Extensive offerings and opening hours has turned this site into an interesting alternative for a great night out. Comprised of three T-laced buildings and a cluster of lifestyle stores designed by Klein Dytham, this spot quells cravings for books, international magazines, music, well-crafted toys, and a decent late night meal. In the main blocks, find categorised reads, a travel counter and stationery on the first floor, a second floor is entirely dedicated to movies, tracks and a library of archived magazines. Eat, drink, read and relax on many seats scattered across the space.

- ⏰ 1F: 0700–0200, 2F: 0900– daily
- 🏠 17–5, Sarugakucho, Shibuya-ku
- ☎ +81 (0)3 37 70 25 25
- 🔗 tsite.jp/daikanyama/

"Take a book and consult it over a coffee at one of the countless shared sitting areas."

– Philip Giordano

51 **SuperDeluxe**
Map D, P.104

Life in this free-and-easy burrow draws designers, architects, and musicians to come eat, drink and think. Opened by Klein Dytham in 2003, the dynamic space multitasks as an art gallery, lounge and creative kitchen that doles out world food alongside free-form dance performance, improv jazz, and PechaKucha nights. The night, on the last Wednesdays of each month, invites creative people to share stories, and has become a popular pastime. On days without performances, the lounge is a welcome spot to drink and read from 7pm-1am.

🕐 Ⓢ *Showtime & ticket price vary with programmes* 🏠 *BIF-3-1-25, Nishiazabu, Minato-ku* 📞 *+81 (0)3 54 12 05 15* 🔗 *www.super-deluxe.com*

"It's the home of PechaKucha night. Check the online schedule, there is something amazing going on most nights."

– Klein Dytham architecture

52 Black List Tokyo
Map D, P.104

Say yes if a Black List member offers to take you to one of these makeshift parties as it guarantees a top-flight night. Playing only the cream of the crop of out-and-out house, high-flying guests from the worlds of art, fashion, media, finance and sports rub shoulders at least once a month at always-fabulous venues where hot, sexy dancers heat up the floor and renowned DJs blast their choice picks. Show-stopping outfits are celebrated!

🏠 Regular venues:
LE.GA: AXALL, BF-7-8-6, Roppongi, Minato-ku
1967: EX Keyakizaka BLD L-Tower, 3F-5-10-25,
Roppongi, Minato-ku
URL *blacklisttokyo.com*

"If you love going out and dancing hard with your Louboutins on, this is the party for you."
– Yuko Fukuba, DDB

53 New York Bar
Map E, P.105

Order a Big Apple-inspired cocktail and sit back to enjoy a glamorous night view of central Tokyo. The landmark venue, located on the 52nd floor of the Park Hyatt Tokyo, where director Sofia Coppola filmed her Academy Award-winning *Lost in Translation* (2003), serves an endless list of premium cognac, vintages and Japanese and world whiskies of varied classes. International musicians play live jazz every night. A cover charge applies from 8pm when the music starts, or from 7pm on Sundays.

🕑 1700-0100 (Th-Sa), -0000 (Su-W)
🏠 Park Hyatt Tokyo, 52F-3-7-1-2, Nishishinjuku, Shinjuku-ku 📞 +81 (0)3 53 23 34 58
🔗 tokyo.park.hyatt.com
✐ Dress code: no sandals, shorts & sportswear

"The night view of Tokyo from here is very beautiful. Go here to chill out, relax and see a different Tokyo."

– MIHO, Saji

54 WOMB

Map A P.102

With an expansive programme of outdoor shows and music festivals, as well as state of the art light and sound system, WOMB is like a scene from Guillermo Arriaga's 2006 movie *Babel*. As the largest concert venue in Shibuya, the four-story venue continues to expand its runaway network of artists, and wows concert-goers with world-class shows, musicians and nationwide festival "Womb Adventure" held every December in Chiba. Despite its size, the venue is hidden on a backstreet, so first-timers should factor in time to track it down.

🕐 **S** *2200 till late (M-Th: lounge only, ¥1,500), 2300 till late (F-Sa, ¥3,500), flexible hours and admission on Sundays* 🏠 *2-16, Maruyamacho, Shibuya-ku* 📞 *+81 (0)3 54 59 00 39* **URL** *www.womb.co.jp* 📎 *20+ w/ photo ID*

"It's a best live concert venue with wonderful music and open-plan floor. Check a map in advance since the entrance may not be immediately obvious."

– Nobuyuki Hanabusa, enra

55 Yako

Map U, P.111

Meaning "night glow" in kanji, oil refineries, power plants, and chemical factories cluster in Kawasaki's Keihin industrial zone, 20km south of central Tokyo. Manmade waterways weave between islands and reclaimed land, where factories rumble and steam clouds and glow-ing lights brighten the darkest nights. Relish the unique sight with a night cruise tour view from Tokyo bay. Trips by the Keihin Ferry set off from Osanbashi (#2).

🏠 Yako, Kawasaki-ku, Kawasaki, Kanagawa
🕐 +81 (0)4 52 01 08 21 🖉 Boat tours (90mins): 1900 (Tu & F), 1830 (Sa–Su & P.H.), ¥3,800/2,200, www.keihinferry.co.jp/event/factory.html

"Yako is my hometown. Enjoy the fantastic views when the graceless industrial area is illuminated by fluorescent light."

– Shunya Hagiwara

56 Trick or Treat Horror Dining
Map D, P.104

Though the surroundings may suggest otherwise, diners are not expected to delve into a bowl of guts, slime or blood. The menu here is the only thing that isn't steeped in horror, instead, it's the setting that will raise the hairs on your back. Candles, witches and skeletons create an eerie mysterious ambience much like entering a film set (Quentin Tarantino and Tim Burton are said to be fans). Try to book your visit during October to coincide with their 'Trick or Treat's Halloween party every year.

🕐 Except P.H.: 1830–0200 (M–Th), –0500 (F–Sa)
🏠 2A-7-16-5, Roppongi, Minato-ku
📞 +81 (0)3 34 03 51 15
🔗 hdaimc14.xsrv.jp/trick_or_treat/top.php

"Come for an unforgettable 'Zombie Night' or a real Halloween!"
– TAKAKO

57 Ebisu Yokocho
Map F, P.105

The twenty-one food outlets on this lively alleyway offer an authentic insight into youthful Japanese culture. Famous for its colourful retro lights and the huge white lantern marking its entrance, Ebisu Yokocho near Ebisu station is affordable and varied. To make the most of the selection, barhop with friends and try the *kushikatsu* (deep-fried kebabs), *okonomiyaki* pancakes and curry-flavoured simmered rafute pork. The atmosphere usually picks up at around 8pm and lasts till 4am, so night owls will find themselves in their element.

🕐 Opening hours vary with shops
🏠 1-7-4, Ebisu, Shibuya-ku
URL www.ebisu-yokocho.com

"Live like a real Japanese here where traditional shopping, entertainment and residents gather in one place."
– Keisuke Matsushima

58 Vampire

Map P, P.110

A swarm of standing room only bars crowds the front of Musashikoyama station, a busy hub that serves up quick tasty drinks and dishes. The bars here are casual, unpretentious and specifically tailored for fun conversation. Vampire is little outlet well versed in sashimi, known especially for its selection of super fresh fish caught daily and sourced locally from the nearby market. The mackerel sashimi is particularly popular, and prices here rarely exceed ¥200.

🕐 1100-2330 daily
🏠 3-20, Koyama, Shinagawa-ku
📞 +81 (0)3 37 85 76 35   🖋 Cash only

"It is so-called 'Sen-Belo' bar, meaning that you can get drunk heavily at just one thousand yen. Japanese call it 'Belo-Belo' (a Japanese mimetic word)."

– Novumichi Tosa, Maywa Denki

59 LOFT/PLUS ONE
Map E, P.105

Feel the vibe of heated discussion at this "live house." A branch of the subculture initiative LOFT Project, the *izakaya*-style club introduces a potpourri of spoken word where comedians, musicians, filmmakers, porn actresses and manga fans come to talk on just about any-thing – from love philosophy to music to ghost stories. Only adults with valid ID are admitted at midnight events, and a minimum order from the kitchen applies.

🕐 Opening hours vary with programmes
🏠 B2F-1-14-7, Kabukicho, Shinjuku-ku
📞 +81 (0)3 32 05 68 64 URL www.loft-prj.co.jp/
PLUSONE 🔖 18+ w/ID for specific shows

"Even if you don't understand Japanese, you can surely experience one aspect of Japan through the audience's enthusiasm towards every performance."
– Mitsuo Murai, Nanarokusha Publishing Co.

60 Mahakala
Map F, P.105

Among the vintage fashion shops and laid-back cafés dotted along the cherry tree-lined Meguro River stands Mahakala, where spirited scarfed men serve up Kansai fare. Highlights include Osakan *Kushikatsu* (deep-fried meat cutlets, seafood or vegetable skewers), Kobe-style *Ikatamayaki* (egg-based savoury pancake grilled with bonito broth and squid) and guinea-fowl sashimi. Wash down the food with a choice of sake, beer, shochu or fruit wine, then wrap up the night with killer puddings, available for dine-in or takeaway.

🕐 1800-0200 (M, W-Sa), -0100 (Su & P.H)
🏠 Maison Aoba 102, 1-17-5, Aobadai, Meguro-ku
📞 +81 (0)3 34 63 51 47
🔗 www.mahakala-nakameguro.com

"Go for Kushikatsu as they recommend."
– Shogo Kishino, 6D

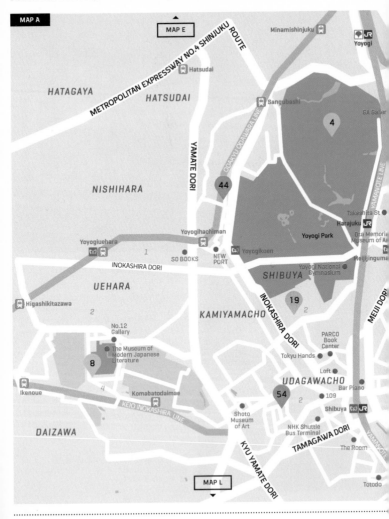

- 4_Meiji Jingu
- 8_Nihon Mingeikan
- 19_NHK Studio Park
- 44_Little Nap COFFEE STAND
- 54_WOMB

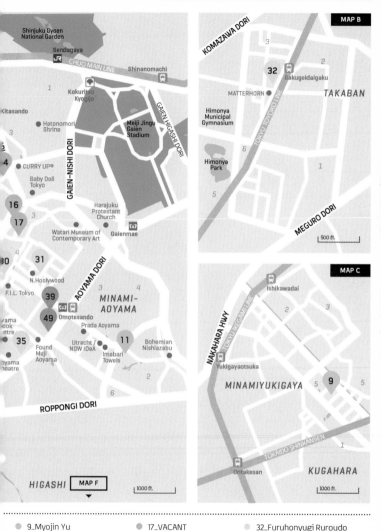

MAP B

MAP C

- 9_Myojin Yu
- 11_Nezu Museum
- 14_UltraSuperNew Gallery
- 16_TOKYO CULTUART by BEAMS
- 17_VACANT
- 30_TRADING MUSEUM COMME des GARÇONS
- 31_CHRISTOPHER NEMETH
- 32_Furuhonyugi Ruroudo
- 35_Farmer's Market at UNU
- 39_Sahsya Kanetanaka
- 49_TWO ROOMS GRILL BAR

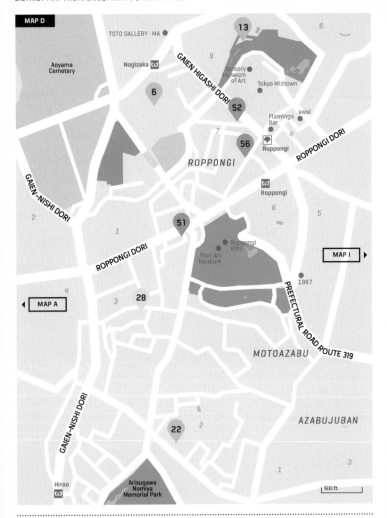

- 6_The National Art Center,Tokyo
- 13_21_21 DESIGN SIGHT
- 22_Kaikai Kiki Gallery
- 51_SuperDeluxe
- 52_Black List Tokyo
- 56_Trick or Treat Horror Dining

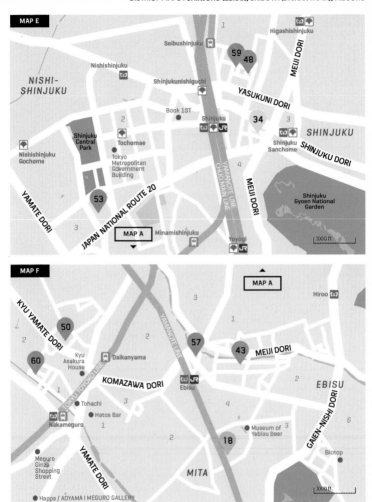

- 18_Tokyo Metropolitan Museum of Photography
- 34_Disk Union Shinjuku Main Store
- 43_TRAUMARIS
- 48_Robot Restaurant
- 50_DAIKANYAMA TSUTAYA BOOKS
- 53_New York Bar
- 57_Ebisu Yokocho
- 59_LOFT/PLUS ONE
- 60_Mahakala

DISTRICT MAPS : **NAKANO, SHINJUKU (SHIMOOCHIAI), MINATO**

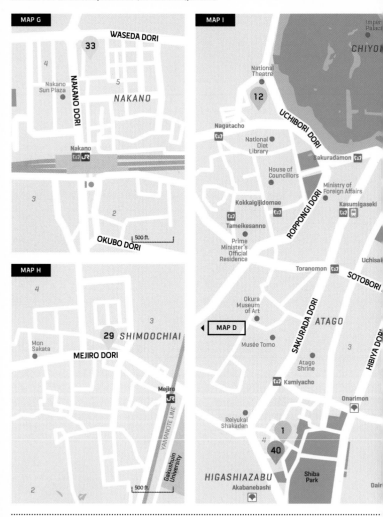

- ● 1_TOKYO TOWER
- ● 12_Saiko Saibansho
- ● 29_Sakata
- ● 33_Nakano Broadway
- ● 40_Tokyo Shiba Tofuya–Ukai

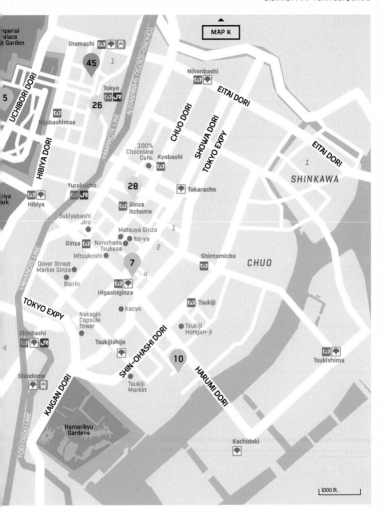

MAP K

- 5_Kokyogaien
- 7_Ginza Kabukiza
- 10_Namiyoke Inari Jinja
- 26_THE SHOP
- 28_HIGASHIYA GINZA
- 45_(marunouchi) HOUSE

DISTRICT MAPS : **ARAKAWA (NIPPORI), TAITO (UENO), CHIYODA (KANDA)**

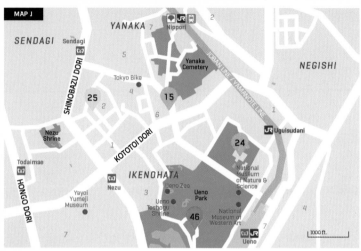

- 15_SCAI THE BATHHOUSE
- 24_Tokyo National Museum
- 25_classico
- 27_TAKEO MIHONCHO HONTEN
- 46_Innsyoutei

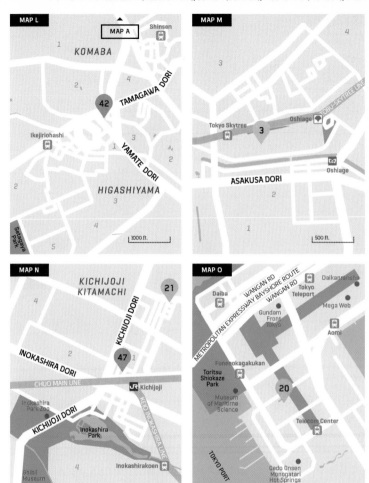

- 3_TOKYO SKYTREE®
- 20_Miraikan
- 21_Art Center Ongoing
- 42_Cafe Grill Bar Taiyo
- 47_Harmonica Yokocho

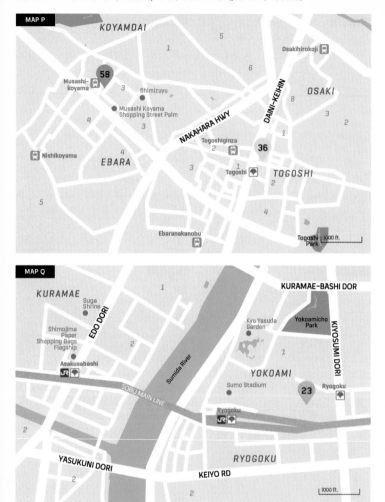

- 23_Edo-Tokyo Museum
- 36_Togoshi Ginza Shotengai
- 58_Vampire

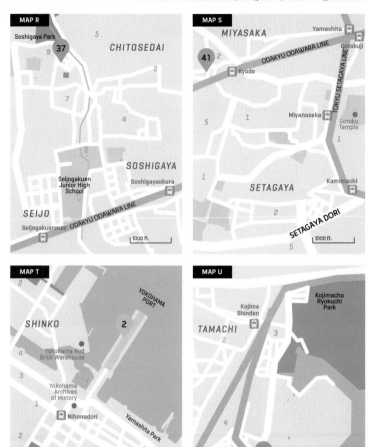

- ● 2_Osanbashi Yokohama
- ● 55_Yako
- ● 37_Seijo 9-chome Cafe
- ● 41_Harubarutei

Accommodations

Hip hostels, fully-equipped apartments & swanky hotels

No journey is perfect without a good night's sleep to recharge. Whether you're backpacking or on a business trip, our picks combine top quality and convenience, whatever your budget.

 < ¥10,000 💵 ¥10,001+

Kangaroo Hotel

Expect a comfy stay at this family-run hotel. Small but sleek, no-frills lodgings are air-conditioned and come with TV, LAN cable, a mini-fridge, single beds or tatami mats. A shared bath, showers and 24hr laundry are located on the first floor. Basic amenities are included but toothbrush and bath towels need to be rented.

🏠 1-21-11, Nihonzutsumi, Taito-ku
📞 +81 (0)3 38 72 85 73 URL kangaroohotel.jp 💲

CLASKA

Japanese design sensibility and western decor fuses at the opulent CLASKA. Gifted designers innovated its 20 guest rooms, including a Weekly Residence where Torafu Architects added eccentric wall cut-outs for storage and hanging clothes. Check out CLASKA's shop for home designs in the same dashing style.

🏠 1-3-18, Chuo-cho, Meguro-Ku
📞 +81 (0)3 37 19 81 21 URL claska.com

Kimi Ryokan

Residing a short walk away from Ikebukuro JR station, Kimi Ryokan is a traditional Japanese inn equipped with tatami mats. The five storeys are accessible by elevator, with a sun-kissed terrace, showers and coin laundry to share. Rooms hold up to five, with Wi-Fi.

🏠 2-36-8, Ikebukuro, Toshima-ku
📞 +81 (0)3 39 71 37 66
URL www.kimiryokan.jp

💲)

Andon Ryokan

🏠 2-34-10, Nihonzutsumi, Taito-ku
📞 +81 (0)3 38 73 86 11
URL www.andon.co.jp

Kamejikan

🏠 3-17-21, Zaimokuza, Kamakura
📞 +81 (0)4 67 25 11 66
URL kamejikan.com

Oakwood Apartments Roppongi Central Tokyo

🏠 3-8-5, Roppongi, Minato-ku
📞 +81 (0)3 54 12 68 00
URL www.oakwoodasia.com
📎 minimum stay spans 30 days

Notes

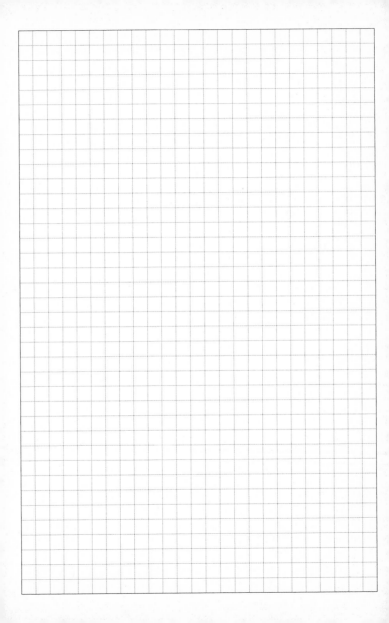

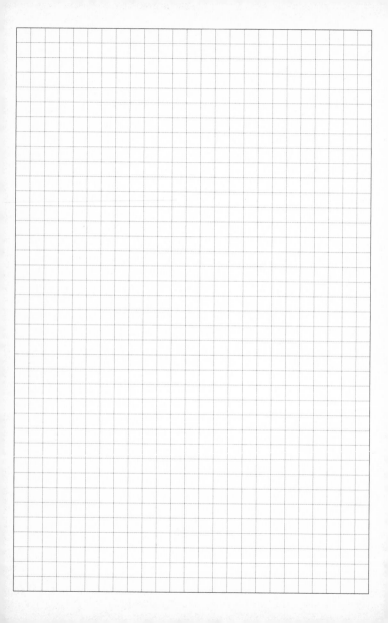

Index

CITIX60

CITIx60: Tokyo

First published and distributed by
viction workshop ltd

viction:ary™

7C Seabright Plaza, 9-23 Shell Street,
North Point, Hong Kong

Url: www.victionary.com
Email: we@victionary.com
🅵 www.facebook.com/victionworkshop
🐦 www.twitter.com/victionary_
🐦 www.weibo.com/victionary

Edited and produced by viction:ary

Concept & art direction: Victor Cheung
Research & editorial: Queenie Ho, Jovan Lip, Caroline Kong
Project coordination: Katherine Wong
Design & map illustration: Cherie Yip

Editing: Elle Kwan
Contributing writer: Monique Todd
Project coordination & translation (JP): Mariko Yokogi
Cover map illustration: Masako Kubo
Count to 10 illustrations: Guillaume Kashima aka Funny Fun
Photography: Martin Holtkamp

© 2014 viction workshop ltd

Content is compiled based on facts available as of February 2014. Travellers
are advised to check for updates from respective locations before your visit.

Second edition
ISBN 978-988-12227-6-3
Printed and bound in China

Acknowledgements

A special thank you to all creatives, photographer(s), editor, producers, com-
panies and organisations for your crucial contributions to our inspiration and
knowledge necessary for the creation of this book. And, to the many whose
names are not credited but have participated in the completion of the book,
we thank you for your input and continuous support all along.

CITIX60
City Guides

CITIx60 is a handpicked list of hot spots that illustrates the spirit of the world's most exhilarating design hubs. From what you see to where you stay, this city guide series leads you to experience the best — the places that only passionate insiders know and go.

Each volume is a unique collaboration with local creatives from selected cities. Known for their accomplishments in fields as varied as advertising, architecture and graphics, fashion, industry and food, music and publishing, these locals are at the cutting edge of what's on and when. Whether it's a one-day stopover or a longer trip, **CITIx60** is your inspirational guide.

Stay tuned for new editions.

City guides available now:

Barcelona
Berlin
London
New York
Paris
Tokyo